Selections from the Islamic legal code
(the *Sharia*) and *Manusmriti*.
Common grounds, common codes.

OPEN WINDOWS: A FEMINIST
RESEARCH CENTER.

Published by

LIES AND BIG FEET

ISBN: 9384281123
ISBN-13: 978-9384281120

PREFATORY NOTE.

There is a section in the *Sharia* (written post 700 AD) that has rules about how women should cover their bodies during prayers:

Issue 797: A woman should cover her entire body while offering prayers, including her head and hair. As a recommended precaution, she should also cover the soles of her feet. It is not necessary for her to cover that part of her face which is washed while performing Wudhu, or the hands up to the wrists, or the upper feet up to the ankles. Nevertheless, in order to ensure that she has covered the obligatory parts of her body adequately, she should also cover a part of the sides of her face as well as lower part of her wrists and the ankles.

Similarly, there are many sections in *Manusmriti* (written around the 2nd-3rd century AD) which codify behaviour for women.

- By a girl, by a young woman, or even by an aged one, nothing must be done independently, even in her own house.
- In childhood a female must be subject to her father, in youth to her husband, when her lord is dead to her sons; a woman must never be independent.
- She must not seek to separate herself from her father, husband, or sons; by leaving them she would

make both (her own and her husband's) families contemptible.

- She must always be cheerful, clever in (the management of her) household affairs, careful in cleaning her utensils, and economical in expenditure.
- By a girl, by a young woman, or even by an aged one, nothing must be done independently, even in her own house.
- She must not seek to separate herself from her father, husband, or sons; by leaving them she would make both (her own and her husband's) families contemptible.
- She must always be cheerful, clever in (the management of her) household affairs, careful in cleaning her utensils, and economical in expenditure.

The intent of these legal texts – both Islamic and Hindu – was to control all aspects of a woman's behaviour.

SECTION I:
SELECTIONS FROM THE
SHARIA:[1]

Islamic laws are seen as being eternal and of divine nature; they are immune from the passage of time. The Koran states:

> When Allah' and His Messenger have decreed a matter, it is not for any believing man or believing woman to have a choice in their affair. And whosoever disobeys Allah and His Messenger has gone astray into clear error. (Surah Al-Ahzaab, 33:36)

Islamic laws deal with many subjects: namely, topics of crime, economics, politics, as well as personal subjects like cleanliness and hygiene, prayers, diet and fasting, hajj, sexual intercourse, etiquette and marriage, amongst other topics.

The Koran consists of more than 6,000 verses, which were collected after the death of the Prophet Mohammed in 632 A.D. and subsequently divided into 114 chapters in a single book.

---

[1] The extracts from the *Sharia* are based on the interpretations of the Fatawa of Ayatullah al Uzma Sayyid Ali al-Husaini Seestani. For the full text, see: http://www.al-islam.org/islamic-laws-ayatullah-ali-al-husayni-al-sistani.

Islamic legal theory emerges from the following texts:

I. the Koran which deals with:

1. Issues of faith like idolatry etc.

2. Laws on rituals like dietary constraints

3. Ethical issues like gambling, fraud

4. Family laws like rules on marriage, status of women, etc. and lastly

5. Civil and criminal laws.

II. The *Sunna* of the prophet which is recorded in the *Hadith*. The *Hadith* and *Sunna* have to be seen as complementing the Koran and consist of the sayings of the Prophet and accounts of his deeds. The *Sunna*, in most ways, is an explanatory model on the Koran, but it may not be interpreted or applied in a manner that is discordant with the Koran.

There are other sources of law: —i.e., ijma', (consensus), qiyas, (analogy), ijtihad, (progressive reasoning by analogy)—we have to remember that the Koran is the primary source, followed by the *Hadith* and *Sunna*.

1 KINDS OF BLOOD SEEN BY WOMEN

[Note: These particular laws on purity and cleanliness reflect an acute desire to control a woman's body, and her biology. The discussions on menstrual blood and cleanliness are quite elaborate to the point of being fetishistic. If a legal code, which functions in a public domain, focuses on what is essentially a private, biologically natural phenomenon, it has the potential of becoming a travesty.]

Kinds of Blood Seen by Women

Istihaza

One type of blood which is seen by women is called *istihaza* and a woman in that state is called *mustahaza*.

Issue 398: *Istihaza* is usually yellowish and cold and is emitted without gush or irritation and is also not thick. It is, however, possible that at times the colour of the blood may be red or dark, and it may also be warm and thick and may be issued with gush and irritation.

Issue 399: There are three kinds of *istihaza* viz. slight (Qalila), medium (Mutawaassita) and excessive (Kathira). Explanation is given below:

I. Little Blood (Qalila)

If the blood remains on the surface of the wool or pad etc., (placed by a woman on her private part) but does not penetrate into it, the *istihaza* is called qalila.

II. Medium Blood (Mutawassita)

If the blood penetrates into the cotton (or pad etc.), even partially, but does not soak the cloth tied on the outer side, the *istihaza* is called mutawassita.

III. Excessive Blood (Kathira)

If the blood penetrates through the cotton, soaking it and the cloth (etc.) around it, the *istihaza* is called kathira.

Rules of *Istihaza*

Issue 400: * In the case of little *istihaza* the a woman should perform separate Wudhu for every prayer and should, as a recommended precaution, wash or change the pad. And if some blood is found on the outer part of her private parts she should make it Clean (tahir/pak) with water.

Issue 401: * In the case of Mutawassita, it is an obligatory precaution for a woman to make one Ghusl every day for her daily prayers, and she should act accordingly to the rules of little *Istihaza* as explained in the foregoing rule. If the state of *Istihaza* began before or just at the time of Fajr prayers, she should do Ghusl before offering Fajr prayers. If she does not do Ghusl intentionally or forgetfully, she should do Ghusl before Zuhr and Asr prayers. And if she misses even that, then she should do Ghusl before praying Maghrib and Isha. This she would do regardless of whether bleeding continues or stops.

Issue 402: * In the case of excessive bleeding the woman should change, as an obligatory precaution, the cotton or pad tied to her private parts or make it Clean (tahir/pak) with water. It is also necessary that she should do one Ghusl for Fajr prayers, one for Zuhr and Asr prayers and once again for Maghrib and Isha prayers. She should offer Asr prayers immediately after Zuhr prayers and if she allowed any lapse of time between them, she should do Ghusl again for Asr prayers. Similarly if she keeps any time gap between Maghrib and Isha prayers, she should do Ghusl again for Isha prayers.

All these rules apply when bleeding is so excessive that it continues soiling the pad etc. But if it takes longer to soil the cotton or pad, and a woman has enough time to pray one or more Salat in between, then, as per obligatory precaution, she would change the pad or wash it to make Clean (tahir/pak) and then do Ghusl only when the cloth covering the pad or cotton is fully soaked.

For example, if a woman praying Salat of Zuhr finds out that the cloth is fully soaked again before the prayers of Asr, she would do Ghusl for Asr prayers.

And if she finds that the flow of blood is slow enough to allow two or more prayers to be offered before the cotton or cloth is totally soiled with blood, there will be no need for Ghusl before the ensuing prayer. For example, if she finds that there is enough time to offer even Maghrib and Isha prayers, before the cloth is fully soaked, she would pray Maghrib and Isha without Ghusl.

In every case, the Ghusl in excessive *Istihaza* does not require Wudhu after it.

Issue 403: If *istihaza* blood is seen before the time for prayers has set in, and the woman has not performed Wudhu or Ghusl for that bleeding, she should perform Wudhu or Ghusl at the time of prayers, even though she may not be mustahaza at that time.

Issue 404: * A woman whose *Istihaza* is medium should first do Ghusl and then Wudhu, as per obligatory precaution. But if a woman with excessive *Istihaza* wishes to do Wudhu, she should do so before the Ghusl.

Issue 405: When a woman who had little *Istihaza* finds out after Fajr prayers that her *Istihaza* has developed into medium one, she will have to do Ghusl for Zuhr and Asr prayers. And if that change occurs after Zuhr, Asr prayers, then she will do a Ghusl for Maghrib and Isha prayers.

Issue 406: * If a woman finds out after Fajr prayers that her little or medium *Istihaza* had developed into an excessive one, and remained in that state, then she should follow the directives given in rule no. 402 in respect of Zuhr, Asr, Maghrib and Isha prayers.

Issue 407: * As explained in rule 402, a woman in excessive *Istihaza* must ensure that there is no time gap between Ghusl and the prayers. Therefore, if such a gap occurs because of doing Ghusl earlier, then that Ghusl will be void, and the woman will have to do Ghusl again. This rule applies to those also who are in medium *Istihaza*.

2 ON MARRIAGE

MARRIAGE:

Issue 2371:* The relation between man and woman becomes lawful by contracting marriage. There are two kinds of marriages:

(i) Permanent marriage

(ii) Fixed-time marriage

In a permanent marriage, the period of matrimony is not fixed, and it is forever. The woman with whom such a marriage is concluded is called da'ima (i.e. a permanent wife).

In a fixed time marriage (Mut'ah), the period of matrimony is fixed, for example, matrimonial relation is contracted with a woman for an hour, or a day, or a month, or a year, or more. However, the period fixed for the marriage should not exceed the span of normal lives of the spouses, because in that case, the marriage will be treated as a permanent one. This sort of fixed time marriage is called Mut'ah or Sigha.

Marriage Formula

Issue 2372: * Whether marriage is permanent or temporary, the formal formula must be pronounced; mere tacit approval and consent, or written agreement, is not sufficient. And the formula (Sigha) of the marriage contract is pronounced either by the man and the woman themselves, or by a person who is appointed by them as their representatives to recite it on their behalf.

Issue 2373: The representative should not necessarily be a male. A woman can also become a representative to pronounce the marriage formula.

Issue 2374: * As long as the woman and the man are not certain that their representative has pronounced the formula, they cannot look at each other as Mahram (like husband and wife), and a mere probable suspicion that the representative might have pronounced the formula is not sufficient. And if the representative says that he has pronounced the formula, but his assertion does not satisfy the parties concerned, it will not be deemed sufficient.

Issue 2375: If a woman appoints a person as her representative so that he may, for example, contract her marriage with a man for ten days, but does not specify the day from which the period of ten days would commence, the representative can contract her marriage with that man for ten days from any day he likes. However, if the representative knows that the woman intends a particular hour or day, he should pronounce the formula according to her intention.

Issue 2376: One person can act as the representative of both sides for reciting the formula of permanent or temporary marriage. It is also permissible that a man may himself become the representative of a woman and contract permanent or temporary marriage with her. However, the recommended precaution is that two separate persons should represent each side, for the formula of marriage contract.

The Method of Pronouncing the Marriage Formula

Issue 2377: * If a woman and a man themselves want to recite the formula of permanent marriage, the woman should first say: Zawwajtuka nafsi 'alas sidaqil ma'lum (i.e. I have made myself your wife on the agreed mahr), and then the man should immediately respond thus: Qabiltut tazwij (i.e. I accept the marriage). In this way, the marriage contract will be in order. And if a woman and a man appoint other person to act as their representatives for pronouncing the formula of marriage, and if, for example, the name of the man is Ahmad and that of the woman is

Fatimah, the representative of the woman should first say: Zawwajtuka muwakkilaka Ahmad muwakkilati Fatimah 'alas sidaqil ma'lum (i.e. I have given to your client Ahmad in marriage my client Fatimah on the agreed mahr) and thereafter the representative of the man should immediately respond thus: Qabiltut tazwijali Muwakkili Ahmad 'alas sidaqil ma'lum (that is, I accepted this matrimonial alliance for my client Ahmad on the agreed Mahr). Now the marriage contract is in order. And, on the basis of recommended precaution, it is necessary that the words uttered by the man should conform with those uttered by the woman; for example, if the woman says: Zawwajituka ...... (i.e. I have made myself your wife) the man should also say: Qabituttazwija ......(i.e. I accept the matrimonial alliance) and not Qabitun Nikaha.

Issue 2378: * It is permissible for a man and a woman to recite the formula of the temporary marriage (Mut'ah), after having agreed on the period of marriage and the amount of Mahr. Hence, if the woman says: Zawwajtuka nafsi fil muddatil ma'lumati 'alal mahril ma'lum (i.e. I have made myself your wife for an agreed period and agreed Mahr), and then the man immediately responds thus: Qabiltu (i.e. I have accepted), the marriage will be in order. And the marriage will also be in order if they appoint other persons to act as their representatives. First, the representative of the woman should say to the representative of the man thus: Matta'tu muwakkilati muwakkilaka fil muddatil ma'lumati 'alal mahril ma'lum (i.e. I have given my client to your client in marriage for the agreed period and the agreed Mahr), and then the representative of the man should immediately respond thus: Qabiltut tazwija li muwakkili hakaza (i.e. I accepted this matrimonial alliance for my client this way).

Conditions of Pronouncing Nikah

Issue 2379: * There are certain conditions for the Nikah recited for marriage. They are as follows:

(i) On the basis of precaution, the formula (Nikah) of marriage contract should be pronounced in correct Arabic. And if the man and the woman cannot pronounce the formula in correct Arabic, they can pronounce the Nikah in any other language, and it is not necessary to appoint any representatives. But the words used in translation must convey strictly the meaning of "Zawwajtu" and "Qabiltu".

(ii) The man and the woman or their representatives, who recite the Nikah, should have the intention of Insha' (i.e. reciting it in a creative sense, making it effective immediately). In other words, if the man and the woman themselves pronounce the formula, the intention of the woman by saying: Zawwajtuka nafsi' should be that she effectively makes herself the wife of the man; and by saying: "Qablitut tazwija" the man effectively accepts her as his wife. And if the representatives of the man and the woman pronounce the Nikah, their intention by saying: 'Zawwajtu' and 'Qablitu' should be that the man and the woman who have appointed them as their representatives, have effectively become husband and wife.

(iii) The person who pronounces the Nikah (whether he pronounces it for himself or has been engaged by some other person as his representative) should be sane, and as a precaution, he should be baligh also.

(iv) If the Nikah is pronounced by the representatives or the guardians of the man and the woman, they should identify the man and the woman by uttering their names or making intelligible signs towards them. Hence, if a person has more than one daughters, and he says to a man: Zawwajtuka Ihda Banati (i.e. I have given away one of my daughters to you as your wife) and the man says: Qabiltu (i.e. I have accepted) the marriage contract is void, because the daughter has not been identified.

(v) The woman and the man should be willing to enter into a matrimonial alliance. If, however, the woman ostensibly displays hesitation while giving her consent, but it is known that in her heart, she is agreeable to the marriage, the marriage is in order.

Issue 2380: If, while reciting the Nikah, even one word is pronounced incorrectly, as a result of which its meaning is changed, the marriage contract would be void.

Issue 2381: * If a person pronouncing Nikah comprehends its general meaning, and has a clear intention of effecting that meaning, the Nikah will be valid. It is not necessary for him to know the exact meaning of each word, or to know the laws of Arabic grammar.

Issue 2382: If Nikah of a woman is pronounced to a man without her consent, but later both man and woman endorse the Nikah, the marriage is in order.

Issue 2383: If the woman and the man, or any one of them, is coerced into matrimony, and they give consent after the Nikah has been pronounced, the marriage is in order, although it is better that the Nikah be repeated.

Issue 2384: * The father and the paternal grandfather can contract a marriage on behalf of his minor son or daughter, or on behalf of an insane son or daughter, if they are baligh. And after the children have become baligh or the insane has become sane, he can endorse or abrogate it, if the contracted marriage involves any moral lapse or scandal. And if the marriage contract does not involve any moral lapse or scandal, but the na-baligh son or daughter calls off the marriage, then as an obligatory precaution, a Talaq or a renewed Nikah, whatever the case may be, must be recited.

Issue 2385: * If a girl has reached the age of bulugh and is virgin and mature (i.e. she can decide what is in her own interest) wishes to marry, she should, obtain permission from her father or paternal grandfather, although she may be looking after her own affairs. It is not, however, necessary for her to obtain permission from her mother or brother.

Issue 2386: * In the following situations, it will not be necessary for a woman to seek the permission of her father or paternal grandfather, before getting married:

(i) If she is not a virgin.

(ii) If she is a virgin, but her father or paternal grandfather refuse to grant permission to her for marrying a man who is compatible to her in the eyes of Shariah, as well as custom.

(iii) If the father and the grandfather are not in any way willing to participate in the marriage.

(iv) If they are not in a capacity to give their consent, like in the case of mental illness etc.

(v) If it is not possible to obtain their permission because of their absence, or such other reasons, and the woman is eager to get married urgently.

Issue 2387: * If the father or the paternal grandfather contracts marriage on behalf of his na-baligh son, the boy, upon attaining bulugh, should pay maintenance of his wife. In fact, he should start paying her maintenance before becoming baligh, when he is able to consummate the marriage. And the wife should not be too young to have any sexual relation with the husband. And in the situation other than these, there is a strong indication that she is entitled to maintenance from the husband, therefore a compromise should be carried out as a precaution.

Issue 2388: * If the father or the paternal grandfather contracts a marriage on behalf of his na-baligh son, they should pay the Mahr if the boy does not own any means, or if either of them undertakes to pay the Mahr himself. In other situations, the father or the paternal grandfather can pay Mahr from the boy's wealth, but it should not exceed the proper usual Mahr customarily given in similar cases. But if the circumstances demand that higher Mahr be paid, they can pay it from the boy's wealth, and not otherwise, unless the boy approves it after having become baligh.

Occasions When Husband or Wife Can Nullify Nikah

Issue 2389: * If the husband comes to know after Nikah that his wife had, at the time of Nikah, any one of the following six deficiencies, he can annul the marriage:

(i) Insanity, even if it is intermittent.

(ii) Leprosy

(iii) Leucoderma

(iv) Blindness

(v) Being crippled, even if it is not to the extent of immobility.

(vi) Presence of flesh or a bone in the woman's uterus, which may or may not obstruct sexual intercourse or pregnancy. And if the husband finds that the wife at the time of Nikah, suffered from 'Ifdha' - meaning that her urinary and menstrual tract have been one, or her menstrual passage and rectum have been one, he cannot annul the marriage. As an obligatory precaution, he will have to pronounce talaq if he wants to dissolve the marriage.

Issue 2390: * A woman can annul the Nikah in the following cases, without obtaining divorce:

(i) If she comes to know that her husband has no male organ.

(ii) If she finds that his penis has been cut off before or after the sexual intercourse.

(iii) If he suffers from a disease which disables him from sexual intercourse, even if that disease was contracted after the Nikah, or before or after the sexual intercourse.

Issue 2390: * In the following situations, if a wife refuses to continue with the matrimony and wishes to dissolve the marriage, then as a matter of precaution, the husband or his guardian will solemnise the divorce:

(i) If she comes to know after the Nikah, that the husband was insane at the time of Nikah; or if he becomes insane after the Nikah, before or after consummation of the marriage.

(ii) If she finds out that at the time of Nikah, the husband had been castrated.

(iii) If she learns that he suffered at the time of Nikah from leprosy or leucoderma.

Note: And if the husband is incapable of sexual intercourse, and she wishes to annul the marriage, it will be necessary for her to approach the Mujtahid or his representative, who may allow the husband a period of one year, and if it is found that he was not able to have sexual intercourse with her or with any other woman, the wife can annul the marriage.

Issue 2391: * If the wife annuls the marriage because of the husband's inability to have sexual intercourse, the husband should give her half of her Mahr. But, if the man or the wife annuls the marriage because of one of the other deficiencies enumerated above, and if the marriage has not been consummated, he will not be liable for anything. But if the marriage was consummated, he should pay her full Mahr. If the husband annuls the marriage due to the deficiencies mentioned in rule 2389, he will not be liable for anything if he has not had sexual intercourse with her. But if he has had sexual relation with her, then he has to pay full Mahr.

4 ON MARRIAGE: Women With Whom Matrimony is Haraam

Women With Whom Matrimony is Haraam

Issue 2393: Matrimonial relation is haraam with women who are one's Mahram, for instance, mother, sister, daughter, paternal aunt, maternal aunt, niece (one's brother's or sister's daughter) and mother-in-law.

Issue 2394: If a man marries a woman, then her mother, her maternal grandmother, her paternal grandmother and all the women as the line ascends are his Mahram, even if he may not have had sexual intercourse with the wife.

Issue 2395: If a person marries a woman, and has sexual intercourse with her, the daughters and grand-daughters (daughters of sons, or of daughters) of the wife and their descendants, as the line goes low, become his Mahram, irrespective of whether they existed at the time of his marriage, or were born later.

Issue 2396: If a man marries a woman, but does not have sexual intercourse with her, the obligatory precaution is that as long as their marriage lasts, he should not marry her daughter.

Issue 2397: The paternal and maternal aunt of a man, and the paternal and maternal aunt of his father, and the paternal and maternal aunt of his paternal grandfather, and the paternal and maternal aunt of his mother, and the paternal and maternal aunt of his maternal grandmother, as the line ascends, are all his Mahram.

Issue 2398: The husband's father and grandfather, however high, are the wife's Mahram. Similarly the husband's sons and the grandsons (son of his sons or of daughters), however low, are her Mahram, regardless of whether they existed at the time of her marriage or were born afterwards.

Issue 2399: If a man marries a woman (whether the marriage be permanent or temporary) he cannot marry her sister, as long as she is his wife.

Issue 2400: If a person gives a revocable divorce to his wife, in the manner which will be explained under the rules relating to 'Divorce', he cannot marry her sister during the

Iddah. But if it is an irrevocable divorce, he can marry her sister. And if it is the Iddah of temporary marriage, the obligatory precaution is that one should not marry his wife's sister during that period.

Issue 2401: A man cannot marry the niece (brother's or sister's daughter) of his wife without her permission. But if he marries his nieces without his wife's permission, and she later consents to the marriage, it will be in order.

Issue 2402: * If the wife learns that her husband has married her niece (brother's daughter or sister's daughter) and keeps quiet, and if she later consents to that marriage, it will be in order. If she does not consent later, the marriage will be void.

Issue 2403: * If before marrying his maternal or paternal aunt's daughter, a person commits incest (sexual intercourse) with her mother, he cannot marry that girl on the basis of precaution.

Issue 2404: * If a person marries his paternal or maternal aunt's daughter, and after having consummated the marriage, commits incest with her mother, this act will not become the cause of their separation. And the same rule applies if he commits incest with her mother after the Nikah, but before having consummated the marriage with her, although the recommended precaution is that in this circumstance he should separate from her by giving her divorce.

Issue 2405: * If a person commits fornication with a woman other than his paternal or maternal aunt, the recommended precaution is that he should not marry her daughter. In fact, if he marries a woman, and commits fornication with her mother before having sexual intercourse with her, the recommended precaution is that he should separate from her, but if he has sexual intercourse with her, and thereafter commits fornication with her mother, it is not necessary for him to get separated from her.

Issue 2406: * A Muslim woman cannot marry a non-Muslim, and a male Muslim also cannot marry a non-Muslim woman who are not Ahlul Kitab. However, there is no harm in contracting temporary marriage with Jewish and Christians women, but the obligatory precaution is that a Muslim should not take them in permanent marriage. There are certain sects like Khawarij, Ghulat and Nawasib who claim to be Muslims, but are classified as non-Muslims. Muslim men and women cannot contract permanent or temporary marriage with them.

Issue 2407: If a person commits fornication with a woman who is in the Iddah of her revocable divorce, as a precaution that woman becomes haraam for him. And if he commits fornication with a woman who is in the Iddah of temporary marriage, or of irrevocable divorce, or in the Iddah of death, he can marry her afterwards, although the recommended precaution is that he should not marry her.

The meaning of revocable divorce and irrevocable divorce, and Iddah of temporary marriage, and Iddah of death, will be explained under the rules relating to 'Divorce'.

Issue 2408: * If a person commits fornication with an unmarried woman and who is not in Iddah, as a precaution, he cannot marry her till he has sought forgiveness from Allah, and repented. But if another person wishes to marry her before she has repented, there is no objection. If a woman is known as a lewd person, it will not be permissible to marry her till she has genuinely repented, and similarly, it is not permissible to marry a man known for his lustful character, till he has genuinely repented. If a man wishes to marry a woman of loose character, he should, as a precaution, wait till she becomes Clean (tahir/pak) from her menses, irrespective of whether he had committed fornication with her, or anyone else had done so.

Issue 2409: If a person contracts Nikah with a woman who is in the Iddah of another man, and if the man and the woman both know, or any one of them knows that the Iddah of the woman has not yet come to an end, and if they also know that marrying a woman during her Iddah is haraam, that woman will become haraam for the man forever, even if after the Nikah the man may not have had sexual intercourse with her.

Issue 2410: If a person contracts Nikah with a woman who is in the Iddah of another man, and has sexual intercourse with her, she becomes haraam for him forever even if he did not know that she was in her Iddah, or did not know that it is haraam to marry a woman during her Iddah.

Issue 2411: * If a person marries a woman knowing that she has a husband, he should get separated from her, and should also not marry her at any time afterwards. And the same rule will apply, as a precaution, if he did not know that the woman was already married, and had sexual intercourse with her after Nikah.

Issue 2412: If a married woman commits adultery, she on the basis of precaution, becomes haraam permanently for the adulterer, but does not become haraam for her husband. And if she does not repent, and persists in her action (i.e. continues to commit adultery), it will be better that her husband divorces her, though he should pay her Mahr.

Issue 2413: In the case of the woman who has been divorced, or a woman who contracted a temporary marriage and her husband forgoes the remaining period of marriage, or if the period of her temporary marriage ends, if she marries after some time, and then doubts whether at the time of her second marriage, the Iddah of her first husband had ended or not, she should ignore her doubt.

Issue 2414: * If a baligh person commits sodomy with a boy , the mother, sister and daughter of the boy become haraam for him. And the same law applies when the person on whom sodomy is committed is an adult male, or when the person committing sodomy is na-baligh. But if one suspects or doubts whether penetration occurred or not, then the said woman would not become haraam.

Issue 2415: * If a person marries the mother or sister of a boy, and commits sodomy with the boy after the marriage, as a precaution, they will become haraam for him.

Issue 2416: If a person who is in the state of Ehram (which is one of the acts to be performed during Hajj) marries a woman, the Nikah is void, and if he knew that it was haraam for him to marry in the state of Ehram, he cannot marry that woman again.

Issue 2417: * If a woman who is in the state of Ehram marries a man who is not in the state of Ehram, her Nikah is void. And if she knew that it was haraam to marry in the state of Ehram, as an obligatory precaution, she should not marry that man thereafter.

Issue 2418: * If a man does not perform Tawafun Nisa (which is one of the acts to be performed during Hajj and Umrah Mufradah) his wife and other women become haraam for him. Also, if a woman does not perform Tawafun Nisa, her husband and other men become haraam for her. But, if they (man or woman) perform Tawafun Nisa later, they become halal.

Issue 2419: * If a person contracts Nikah with a non-baligh girl, it is haraam to have sexual intercourse before she has completed her nine years. But if he commits sexual intercourse with her, she will not be haraam for him when she becomes baligh, even if she may have suffered Ifza (which has been described in rule 2389), though as a precaution, he should divorce her.

Issue 2420: A woman who is divorced three times, becomes haraam for her husband. But, if she marries another man, subject to the conditions which will be mentioned under the rules pertaining to 'divorce', her first husband can marry her again after her second husband dies, or divorces her, and she completes the period of Iddah.

5 PERMANENT MARRIAGE

Rules Regarding Permanent Marriage

Issue 2421: * For a woman with whom permanent marriage is contracted, it is haraam to go out of the house without the permission of her husband, though her leaving may not violate the rights of the husband. Also she should submit herself to his sexual desires, and should not prevent him from having sexual intercourse with her, without justifiable excuse. And as long as she does not fail in her duties, it is obligatory on the husband to provide for her food, clothes and housing. And if he does not provide the same, regardless of whether he is able to provide them or not, he remains indebted to the wife.

Issue 2422: * If the wife does not fulfil her matrimonial duties towards her husband, she will not be entitled for the food, clothes or housing, even if she continues to live with him. But if she refuses to obey occasionally, the common verdict is that even then she cannot claim any entitlement from her husband. But this verdict is a matter of Ishkal. In any case, there is no doubt that she does not forfeit her Mahr.

Issue 2423: Man has no right to compel his wife to render household services.

Issue 2424: * The travelling expenses incurred by the wife must be borne by the husband, if they exceed her expenses at home, and if she had travelled with the husband's permission. But the fares for travel by car or by air etc. and other expenses, which are necessary for a journey, will be borne by the wife, except when the husband is himself inclined to take her along with him on a journey, in which case he will bear her expenses also.

Issue 2425: * If the husband who is responsible for the wife's maintenance, does not provide her the same, she can draw her expenses from his property without his permission. And if this is not possible, and she is obliged to earn her livelihood, and she cannot take her case to the Mujtahid, who would compel him (even by threatening him with imprisonment) to pay the maintenance, it will not be obligatory upon her to obey her husband while she is engaged in earning her livelihood.

Issue 2426: * If a man, for example, has two wives and spends one night with one of them, it is obligatory on him to spend anyone of four nights with the other as well; in situation other than this, it is not obligatory on a man to stay with his wife. Of course, it is necessary that he should not totally forsake living with the wife. And as a precaution, a man should spend one night out of every four with his permanent wife.

Issue 2427: * It is not permissible for the husband to abandon sexual intercourse with his youthful, permanent wife for more than 4 months, except when sexual intercourse is harmful to him, or involves unusually more effort, or when the wife herself agrees to avoid it, or if a prior stipulation to that effect was made at the time of Nikah by the husband. And in this rule, there is no difference between the situations when the husband is present, or on a journey, or whether she is a wife by permanent or temporary marriage.

Issue 2428: If Mahr is not fixed in a permanent marriage, the marriage is in order. And in such case, if the husband has sexual intercourse with the wife, he should pay her proper Mahr which would be in accordance with the Mahr usually paid to women of her category. As regards temporary marriage, however, if Mahr is not fixed the marriage is void.

Issue 2429: If at the time of Nikah for permanent marriage, no time is fixed for paying Mahr, the wife can prevent her husband from having sexual intercourse with her before receiving Mahr, irrespective of whether the husband is or is not able to pay it. But if she once agrees to have sexual intercourse before taking Mahr, and her husband has sexual intercourse with her, then she cannot prevent him afterwards from having sexual intercourse without a justifiable excuse.

6 TEMPORARY MARRIAGE

Mut'ah (Temporary Marriage)

Issue 2430: Contracting a temporary marriage with a woman is in order, even if it may not be for the sake of any sexual pleasure.

Issue 2431: The obligatory precaution is that a husband should not avoid having sexual intercourse for more than four months with a wife of temporary marriage.

Issue 2432: * If a woman with whom temporary marriage is contracted, makes a condition that her husband will not have sexual intercourse with her, the marriage as well as the condition imposed by her will be valid, and the husband can then derive only other pleasures from her. However, if she agrees to sexual intercourse later, her husband can have sexual intercourse with her, and this rule applies to permanent marriage as well.

Issue 2433: A woman with whom temporary marriage is contracted, is not entitled to subsistence even if she becomes pregnant.

Issue 2434: * A woman with whom temporary marriage is contracted, is not entitled to share the conjugal bed of her husband, and does not inherit from him, and the husband, too, does not inherit from her. However, if one or both lay down a condition regarding inheriting each other, such a stipulation is a matter of Ishkal as far as its validity is concerned, but even then, precaution should be exercised by putting it into effect.

Issue 2435: If a woman with whom temporary marriage is contracted, did not know that she was not entitled to any subsistence and sharing her husband's conjugal bed, still her marriage will be valid, and inspite of this lack of knowledge, she has no right to claim anything from her husband.

Issue 2436: * If a wife of temporary marriage goes out of the house without the permission of her husband, and the right of the husband is in anyway violated, it is haraam for her to leave. And if the right of her husband remains protected, it is a recommended precaution that she should not leave the house without his permission.

Issue 2437: * If a woman empowers a man that he may contract a temporary marriage with her for a fixed period, and against a specified amount of Mahr, and instead, that man contracts a permanent marriage with her, or contracts a temporary marriage with her without specifying the time or amount of Mahr, the marriage will be void. But if the woman consents to it on understanding the position, then the marriage will be valid.

Issue 2438: In order to become Mahram (with whom marriage contract becomes haraam and is treated to be one of the close relatives), a father or a paternal grandfather can contract the marriage of his na-baligh son or daughter with another person for a short period, provided that it does not involve any scandal or moral lapse. However, if they marry a minor boy or a girl who is not in anyway able to derive any sexual pleasure during the period from the spouse, then the validity of such a marriage is a matter of Ishkal.

Issue 2439: If the father or the paternal grandfather of an absent child, marry it to someone for the sake of becoming Mahram, not knowing whether the child is alive or dead, the purpose will be achieved only if during the period fixed for marriage, the child can become capable of consummating marriage. If it later transpires that it was not alive at the time the marriage was contracted, it will be considered void, and the people who had apparently become Mahram will all become Na-Mahram.

7 DIVORCE

Divorce

Issue 2507: * A man who divorces his wife must be adult and sane, but if a boy of ten years of age divorces his wife, precaution must be exercised. Similarly, a man should divorce of his own free will, therefore, if someone compels him to divorce his wife, that divorce will be void. It is also necessary that a man seriously intends to divorce; therefore, if he pronounces the formula of divorce jokingly, the divorce will not be valid.

Issue 2508: It is necessary that at the time of divorce, wife is Clean (tahir/pak) from Haidth and Nifas, and that the husband should not have had sexual intercourse with her during that period.

Issue 2509: * It is valid to divorce a woman even if she is in Haidh or Nifas in the following circumstances:

(i) If the husband has not had sexual intercourse with her after marriage.

(ii) If it is known that she is pregnant. And if this fact is not known and the husband divorces her during Haidh, and he comes to know later that she was pregnant, that divorce will be valid, and as a recommended precaution he should divorce her again.

(iii) If due to the husband's absence or imprisonment, he is not able to ascertain whether or not she is Clean (tahir/pak) from Haidth or Nifas. But in this case, as an obligatory precaution, man must wait for at least one month after separation from his wife and then divorce.

Issue 2510: If a man thinks that his wife is Clean (tahir/pak) from Haidh and divorces her, but it transpires later that at the time of divorce she was in the state of Haidh, the divorce is void. And if he thinks that she is in the state of Haidh and divorces her, and it is later known that she was Clean (tahir/pak), the divorce is in order.

Issue 2511: * If a person who knows that his wife is in Haidh or Nifas, is separated from her, like when he proceeds on a journey, and wishes to divorce her, he should wait till such time when he becomes sure that his wife must have become Clean (tahir/pak) from her Haidh or Nifas. Thereafter, having known that she is Clean (tahir/pak), he can divorce her. And if he is in doubt he will act according to rule no. 2509 for precaution.

Issue 2512: * If a man who is separated from his wife wishes to divorce her and can acquire information as to whether or not she is in the state of Haidh or Nifas, even if that information is based on her habit, or any other signs known in Shariah, if he divorces her and later finds out that his information was wrong, the divorce will be void.

Issue 2513: * If a man has sexual intercourse with his wife during her Clean (tahir/pak) period, and then wishes to divorce her, he should wait till she enters into Haidh again and becomes Clean (tahir/pak). But if the wife has not completed her ninth year, or if she is pregnant, she can be divorced after the sexual intercourse. The same rule applies to a wife in menopause. The meaning of menopause has been explained in rule no. 2457).

Issue 2514: * If a person has sexual intercourse with a woman during her Clean (tahir/pak) period and divorces her during the same period, and if it transpires later that she was pregnant at the time of divorce, the divorce will be void. As a recommended precaution, he should divorce her again.

Issue 2515: * If a person had sexual intercourse with his wife during her Clean (tahir/pak) period, and then separated from her, like, if he proceeded on journey and wishes to divorce her then, not knowing whether she is Clean (tahir/pak) or not, he should wait till such time when the wife enters into the state of Haidh and becomes Clean (tahir/pak) once again. And, as an obligatory precaution, this period should not be less than one month.

Issue 2516: * If a man wishes to divorce his wife who does see blood of Haidh at all by habit, or because of some disease, while other women of her age habitually see Haidh, he should refrain from having sexual intercourse with her for three months from the time he has had the intercourse, and then divorce her.

SECTION II:

Selections from *Manusmriti.*

By the 5th century AD, *Manava Dharmasastra*, was a well known treatise on Hindu dharma. Sir William Jones translated it in 1794, and the text that has been used here is George Buhler's translation.

No single author can be seen as the sole composer of the text; in fact, *Manava Dharma* has to be seen as a composition that lasted several centuries, and a result of a "gradual process at the hands of anonymous and successive compliers, editors, and copyists." The text was a compilation of proverbial sayings, moral dictates and legal theories which were extant at that time period. It has also been argued that there was a single author of the text.

This treatise was written around the 2nd-3rd century AD. and is divided into 12 chapters.

8 CHAPTER 1

1. The great sages approached Manu, who was seated with a collected mind, and, having duly worshipped him, spoke as follows:

2. 'Deign, divine one, to declare to us precisely and in due order the sacred laws of each of the (four chief) castes (varna) and of the intermediate ones.

87. But in order to protect this universe He, the most resplendent one, assigned separate (duties and) occupations to those who sprang from his mouth, arms, thighs, and feet.

88. To Brahmanas he assigned teaching and studying (the Veda), sacrificing for their own benefit and for others, giving and accepting (of alms).

89. The Kshatriya he commanded to protect the people, to bestow gifts, to offer sacrifices, to study (the Veda), and to abstain from attaching himself to sensual pleasures;

90. The Vaisya to tend cattle, to bestow gifts, to offer sacrifices, to study (the Veda), to trade, to lend money, and to cultivate land.

91. One occupation only the lord prescribed to the Sudra, to serve meekly even these (other) three castes.

92. Man is stated to be purer above the navel (than below); hence the Self-existent (Svayambhu) has declared the purest (part) of him (to be) his mouth.

93. As the Brahmana sprang from (Brahman's) mouth, as he was the first-born, and as he possesses the Veda, he is by right the lord of this whole creation.

94. For the Self-existent (Svayambhu), having performed austerities, produced him first from his own mouth, in order that the offerings might be conveyed to the gods and manes and that this universe might be preserved

95. What created being can surpass him, through whose mouth the gods continually consume the sacrificial viands and the manes the offerings to the dead?

96. Of created beings the most excellent are said to be those which are animated; of the animated, those which subsist by intelligence; of the intelligent, mankind; and of men, the Brahmanas;

97. Of Brahmanas, those learned (in the Veda); of the learned, those who recognise (the necessity and the manner of performing the prescribed duties); of those who possess this knowledge, those who perform them; of the performers, those who know the Brahman.

98. The very birth of a Brahmana is an eternal incarnation of the sacred law; for he is born to (fulfil) the sacred law, and becomes one with Brahman.

99. A Brahmana, coming into existence, is born as the highest on earth, the lord of all created beings, for the protection of the treasury of the law.

100. Whatever exists in the world is, the property of the Brahmana; on account of the excellence of his origin The Brahmana is, indeed, entitled to all.

101. The Brahmana eats but his own food, wears but his own apparel, bestows but his own in alms; other mortals subsist through the benevolence of the Brahmana.

102. In order to clearly settle his duties those of the other (castes) according to their order, wise Manu sprung from the Self-existent, composed these Institutes (of the sacred Law).

103. A learned Brahmana must carefully study them, and he must duly instruct his pupils in them, but nobody else (shall do it).

104. A Brahmana who studies these Institutes (and) faithfully fulfils the duties (prescribed therein), is never tainted by sins, arising from thoughts, words, or deeds.

105. He sanctifies any company (which he may enter), seven ancestors and seven descendants, and he alone deserves (to possess) this whole earth.

106. (To study) this (work) is the best means of securing welfare, it increases understanding, it procures fame and long life, it (leads to) supreme bliss.

107. In this (work) the sacred law has been fully stated as well as the good and bad qualities of (human) actions and the immemorial rule of conduct, (to be followed) by all the four castes (varna).

108. The rule of conduct is transcendent law, whether it be taught in the revealed texts or in the sacred tradition; hence a twice-born man who possesses regard for himself, should be always careful to (follow) it.

109. A Brahmana who departs from the rule of conduct, does not reap the fruit of the Veda, but he who duly follows it, will obtain the full reward.

110. The sages who saw that the sacred law is thus grounded on the rule of conduct, have taken good conduct to be the most excellent root of all austerity.

111. The creation of the universe, the rule of the sacraments, the ordinances of studentship, and the respectful behaviour (towards Gurus), the most excellent rule of bathing (on return from the teacher's house),

112. (The law of) marriage and the description of the (various) marriage-rites, the regulations for the great sacrifices and the eternal rule of the funeral sacrifices,

113. The description of the modes of (gaining) subsistence and the duties of a Snataka, (the rules regarding) lawful and forbidden food, the purification of men and of things,

114. The laws concerning women, (the law) of hermits, (the manner of gaining) final emancipation and (of) renouncing the world, the whole duty of a king and the manner of deciding lawsuits,

115. The rules for the examination of witnesses, the laws concerning husband and wife, the law of (inheritance and) division, (the law concerning) gambling and the removal of (men nocuous like) thorns,

116. (The law concerning) the behaviour of Vaisyas and Sudras, the origin of the mixed castes, the law for all castes in times of distress and the law of penances,

117. The threefold course of transmigrations, the result of (good or bad) actions, (the manner of attaining) supreme bliss and the examination of the good and bad qualities of actions,

118. The primeval laws of countries, of castes (gati), of families, and the rules concerning heretics and companies (of traders and the like)- (all that) Manu has declared in these Institutes.

119. As Manu, in reply to my questions, formerly promulgated these Institutes, even so learn ye also the (whole work) from me.

67. The nuptial ceremony is stated to be the Vedic sacrament for women (and to be equal to the initiation), serving the husband (equivalent to) the residence in (the house of the) teacher, and the household duties (the same) as the (daily) worship of the sacred fire.

Chapter 3.

2. (A student) who has studied in due order the three Vedas, or two, or even one only, without breaking the (rules of) studentship, shall enter the order of householders.

3. He who is famous for (the strict performance of) his duties and has received his heritage, the Veda, from his father, shall be honoured, sitting on a couch and adorned with a garland, with (the present of) a cow (and the honey-mixture).

4. Having bathed, with the permission of his teacher, and performed according to the rule the Samavartana (the rite on returning home), a twice-born man shall marry a wife of equal caste who is endowed with auspicious (bodily) marks.

5. A damsel who is neither a Sapinda on the mother's side, nor belongs to the same family on the father's side, is recommended to twice-born men for wedlock and conjugal union.

6. In connecting himself with a wife, let him carefully avoid the ten following families, be they ever so great, or rich in kine, horses, sheep, grain, or (other) property,

7. (Viz.) one which neglects the sacred rites, one in which no male children (are born), one in which the Veda is not studied, one (the members of) which have thick hair on the body, those which are subject to hemorrhoids, phthisis, weakness of digestion, epilepsy, or white or black leprosy.

8. Let him not marry a maiden (with) reddish (hair), nor one who has a redundant member, nor one who is sickly, nor one either with no hair (on the body) or too much, nor one who is garrulous or has red (eyes),

9. Nor one named after a constellation, a tree, or a river, nor one bearing the name of a low caste, or of a mountain, nor one named after a bird, a snake, or a slave, nor one whose name inspires terror.

10. Let him wed a female free from bodily defects, who has an agreeable name, the (graceful) gait of a Hamsa or of an elephant, a moderate (quantity of) hair on the body and on the head, small teeth, and soft limbs.

11. But a prudent man should not marry (a maiden) who has no brother, nor one whose father is not known, through fear lest (in the former case she be made) an appointed daughter (and in the latter) lest (he should commit) sin.

12. For the first marriage of twice-born men (wives) of equal caste are recommended; but for those who through desire proceed (to marry again) the following females, (chosen) according to the (direct) order (of the castes), are most approved.

13. It is declared that a Sudra woman alone (can be) the wife of a Sudra, she and one of his own caste (the wives) of a Vaisya, those two and one of his own caste (the wives) of a Kshatriya, those three and one of his own caste (the wives) of a Brahmana.

14. A Sudra woman is not mentioned even in any (ancient) story as the (first) wife of a Brahmana or of a Kshatriya, though they lived in the (greatest) distress.

15. Twice-born men who, in their folly, wed wives of the low (Sudra) caste, soon degrade their families and their children to the state of Sudras.

16. According to Atri and to (Gautama) the son of Utathya, he who weds a Sudra woman becomes an outcast, according to Saunaka on the birth of a son, and according to Bhrigu he who has (male) offspring from a (Sudra female, alone).

17. A Brahmana who takes a Sudra wife to his bed, will (after death) sink into hell; if he begets a child by her, he will lose the rank of a Brahmana.

18. The manes and the gods will not eat the (offerings) of that man who performs the rites in honour of the gods, of the manes, and of guests chiefly with a (Sudra wife's) assistance, and such (a man) will not go to heaven.

19. For him who drinks the moisture of a Sudra's lips, who is tainted by her breath, and who begets a son on her, no expiation is prescribed.

20. Now listen to (the) brief (description of) the following eight marriage-rites used by the four castes (varna) which partly secure benefits and partly produce evil both in this life and after death.

21. (They are) the rite of Brahman (Brahma), that of the gods (Daiva), that of the Rishis (Arsha), that of Pragapati (Pragapatya), that of the Asuras (Asura), that of the Gandharvas (Gandharva), that of the Rhashasas (Rakshasa), and that of the Pisakas (Paisaka).

22. Which is lawful for each caste (varna) and which are the virtues or faults of each (rite), all this I will declare to you, as well as their good and evil results with respect to the offspring.

23. One may know that the first six according to the order (followed above) are lawful for a Brahmana, the four last for a Kshatriya, and the same four, excepting the Rakshasa rite, for a Vaisya and a Sudra.

24. The sages state that the first four are approved (in the case) of a Brahmana, one, the Rakshasa (rite in the case) of a Kshatriya, and the Asura (marriage in that) of a Vaisya and of a Sudra.

25. But in these (Institutes of the sacred law) three of the five (last) are declared to be lawful and two unlawful; the Paisaka and the Asura (rites) must never be used.

26. For Kshatriyas those before-mentioned two rites, the Gandharva and the Rakshasa, whether separate or mixed, are permitted by the sacred tradition.

27. The gift of a daughter, after decking her (with costly garments) and honouring (her by presents of jewels), to a man learned in the Veda and of good conduct, whom (the father) himself invites, is called the Brahma rite.

28. The gift of a daughter who has been decked with ornaments, to a priest who duly officiates at a sacrifice, during the course of its performance, they call the Daiva rite.

29. When (the father) gives away his daughter according to the rule, after receiving from the bridegroom, for (the fulfilment of) the sacred law, a cow and a bull or two pairs, that is named the Arsha rite.

30. The gift of a daughter (by her father) after he has addressed (the couple) with the text, 'May both of you perform together your duties,' and has shown honour (to the bridegroom), is called in the Smriti the Pragapatya rite.

31. When (the bridegroom) receives a maiden, after having given as much wealth as he can afford, to the kinsmen and to the bride herself, according to his own will, that is called the Asura rite.

32. The voluntary union of a maiden and her lover one must know (to be) the Gandharva rite, which springs from desire and has sexual intercourse for its purpose.

33. The forcible abduction of a maiden from her home, while she cries out and weeps, after (her kinsmen) have been slain or wounded and (their houses) broken open, is called the Rakshasa rite.

34. When (a man) by stealth seduces a girl who is sleeping, intoxicated, or disordered in intellect, that is the eighth, the most base and sinful rite of the Pisakas.

35. The gift of daughters among Brahmanas is most approved, (if it is preceded) by (a libation of) water; but in the case of other castes (it may be performed) by (the expression of) mutual consent.

36. Listen now to me, ye Brahmanas, while I fully declare what quality has been ascribed by Manu to each of these marriage-rites.

37. The son of a wife wedded according to the Brahma rite, if he performs meritorious acts, liberates from sin ten ancestors, ten descendants and himself as the twenty-first.

38. The son born of a wife, wedded according to the Daiva rite, likewise (saves) seven ancestors and seven descendants, the son of a wife married by the Arsha rite

three (in the ascending and descending lines), and the son of a wife married by the rite of Ka (Pragapati) six (in either line).

39. From the four marriages, (enumerated) successively, which begin with the Brahma rite spring sons, radiant with knowledge of the Veda and honoured by the Sishtas (good men).

40. Endowed with the qualities of beauty and goodness, possessing wealth and fame, obtaining as many enjoyments as they desire and being most righteous, they will live a hundred years.

41. But from the remaining (four) blamable marriages spring sons who are cruel and speakers of untruth, who hate the Veda and the sacred law.

42. In the blameless marriages blameless children are born to men, in blamable (marriages) blamable (offspring); one should therefore avoid the blamable (forms of marriage).

43. The ceremony of joining the hands is prescribed for (marriages with) women of equal caste (varna); know that the following rule (applies) to weddings with females of a different caste (varna).

44. On marrying a man of a higher caste a Kshatriya bride must take hold of an arrow, a Vaisya bride of a goad, and a Sudra female of the hem of the (bridegroom's) garment.

45. Let (the husband) approach his wife in due season, being constantly satisfied with her (alone); he may also,

being intent on pleasing her, approach her with a desire for conjugal union (on any day) excepting the Parvans.

46. Sixteen (days and) nights (in each month), including four days which differ from the rest and are censured by the virtuous, (are called) the natural season of women.

47. But among these the first four, the eleventh and the thirteenth are (declared to be) forbidden; the remaining nights are recommended.

48. On the even nights sons are conceived and daughters on the uneven ones; hence a man who desires to have sons should approach his wife in due season on the even (nights).

49. A male child is produced by a greater quantity of male seed, a female child by the prevalence of the female; if (both are) equal, a hermaphrodite or a boy and a girl; if (both are) weak or deficient in quantity, a failure of conception (results).

50. He who avoids women on the six forbidden nights and on eight others, is (equal in chastity to) a student, in whichever order he may live.

51. No father who knows (the law) must take even the smallest gratuity for his daughter; for a man who, through avarice, takes a gratuity, is a seller of his offspring.

52. But those (male) relations who, in their folly, live on the separate property of women, (e.g. appropriate) the beasts of burden, carriages, and clothes of women, commit sin and will sink into hell.

53. Some call the cow and the bull (given) at an Arsha wedding 'a gratuity;' (but) that is wrong, since (the acceptance of) a fee, be it small or great, is a sale (of the daughter).

54. When the relatives do not appropriate (for their use) the gratuity (given), it is not a sale; (in that case) the (gift) is only a token of respect and of kindness towards the maidens.

55. Women must be honoured and adorned by their fathers, brothers, husbands, and brothers-in-law, who desire (their own) welfare.

56. Where women are honoured, there the gods are pleased; but where they are not honoured, no sacred rite yields rewards.

57. Where the female relations live in grief, the family soon wholly perishes; but that family where they are not unhappy ever prospers.

58. The houses on which female relations, not being duly honoured, pronounce a curse, perish completely, as if destroyed by magic.

59. Hence men who seek (their own) welfare, should always honour women on holidays and festivals with (gifts of) ornaments, clothes, and (dainty) food.

60. In that family, where the husband is pleased with his wife and the wife with her husband, happiness will assuredly be lasting.

61. For if the wife is not radiant with beauty, she will not attract her husband; but if she has no attractions for him, no children will be born.

62. If the wife is radiant with beauty, the whole house is bright; but if she is destitute of beauty, all will appear dismal.

63. By low marriages, by omitting (the performance of) sacred rites, by neglecting the study of the Veda, and by irreverence towards Brahmanas, (great) families sink low.

64. By (practising) handicrafts, by pecuniary transactions, by (begetting) children on Sudra females only, by (trading in) cows, horses, and carriages, by (the pursuit of) agriculture and by taking service under a king,

65. By sacrificing for men unworthy to offer sacrifices and by denying (the future rewards for good) works, families, deficient in the (knowledge of the) Veda, quickly perish.

66. But families that are rich in the knowledge of the Veda, though possessing little wealth, are numbered among the great, and acquire great fame.

67. With the sacred fire, kindled at the wedding, a householder shall perform according to the law the domestic ceremonies and the five (great) sacrifices, and (with that) he shall daily cook his food.

68. A householder has five slaughter-houses (as it were, viz.) the hearth, the grinding-stone, the broom, the pestle and mortar, the water-vessel, by using which he is bound (with the fetters of sin).

69. In order to successively expiate (the offences committed by means) of all these (five) the great sages have prescribed for householders the daily (performance of the five) great sacrifices.

70. Teaching (and studying) is the sacrifice (offered) to Brahman, the (offerings of water and food called) Tarpana the sacrifice to the manes, the burnt oblation the sacrifice offered to the gods, the Bali offering that offered to the Bhutas, and the hospitable reception of guests the offering to men.

71. He who neglects not these five great sacrifices, while he is able (to perform them), is not tainted by the sins (committed) in the five places of slaughter, though he constantly lives in the (order of) house (-holders).

72. But he who does not feed these five, the gods, his guests, those whom he is bound to maintain, the manes, and himself, lives not, though he breathes.

73. They call (these) five sacrifices also, Ahuta, Huta, Prahuta, Brahmya-huta, and Prasita.

74. Ahuta (not offered in the fire) is the muttering (of Vedic texts), Huta the burnt oblation (offered to the gods), Prahuta (offered by scattering it on the ground) the Bali offering given to the Bhutas, Brahmya-huta (offered in the digestive fire of Brahmanas), the respectful reception of Brahmana (guests), and Prasita (eaten) the (daily oblation to the manes, called) Tarpana.

75. Let (every man) in this (second order, at least) daily apply himself to the private recitation of the Veda, and also

to the performance of the offering to the gods; for he who is diligent in the performance of sacrifices, supports both the movable and the immovable creation.

76. An oblation duly thrown into the fire, reaches the sun; from the sun comes rain, from rain food, therefrom the living creatures (derive their subsistence).

77. As all living creatures subsist by receiving support from air, even so (the members of) all orders subsist by receiving support from the householder.

78. Because men of the three (other) orders are daily supported by the householder with (gifts of) sacred knowledge and food, therefore (the order of) householders is the most excellent order.

150. Manu has declared that those Brahmanas who are thieves, outcasts, eunuchs, or atheists are unworthy (to partake) of oblations to the gods and manes.

151. Let him not entertain at a Sraddha one who wears his hair in braids (a student), one who has not studied (the Veda), one afflicted with a skin-disease, a gambler, nor those who sacrifice for a multitude (of sacrificers).

152. Physicians, temple-priests, sellers of meat, and those who subsist by shop-keeping must be avoided at sacrifices offered to the gods and to the manes.

153. A paid servant of a village or of a king, man with deformed nails or black teeth, one who opposes his teacher, one who has forsaken the sacred fire, and a usurer;

154. One suffering from consumption, one who subsists by tending cattle, a younger brother who marries or kindles the sacred fire before the elder, one who neglects the five great sacrifices, an enemy of the Brahmana race, an elder brother who marries or kindles the sacred fire after the younger, and one who belongs to a company or corporation,

155. An actor or singer, one who has broken the vow of studentship, one whose (only or first) wife is a Sudra female, the son of a remarried woman, a one-eyed man, and he in whose house a paramour of his wife (resides);

156. He who teaches for a stipulated fee and he who is taught on that condition, he who instructs Sudra pupils and he whose teacher is a Sudra, he who speaks rudely, the son of an adulteress, and the son of a widow,

157. He who forsakes his mother, his father, or a teacher without a (sufficient) reason, he who has contracted an alliance with outcasts either through the Veda or through a marriage,

158. An incendiary, a prisoner, he who eats the food given by the son of an adulteress, a seller of Soma, he who undertakes voyages by sea, a bard, an oil-man, a suborner to perjury,

159. He who wrangles or goes to law with his father, the keeper of a gambling-house, a drunkard, he who is afflicted with a disease (in punishment of former) crimes, he who is accused of a mortal sin, a hypocrite, a seller of substances used for flavouring food,

160. A maker of bows and of arrows, he who lasciviously dallies with a brother's widow, the betrayer of a friend, one who subsists by gambling, he who learns (the Veda) from his son,

35. Keeping his hair, nails, and beard clipped, subduing his passions by austerities, wearing white garments and (keeping himself) pure, he shall be always engaged in studying the Veda and (such acts as are) conducive to his welfare.

36. He shall carry a staff of bamboo, a pot full of water, a sacred string, a bundle of Kusa grass, and (wear) two bright golden ear-rings.

37. Let him never look at the sun, when he sets or rises, is eclipsed or reflected in water, or stands in the middle of the sky.

38. Let him not step over a rope to which a calf is tied, let him not run when it rains, and let him not look at his own image in water; that is a settled rule.

39. Let him pass by (a mound of) earth, a cow, an idol, a Brahmana, clarified butter, honey, a crossway, and well-known trees, turning his right hand towards them.

40. Let him, though mad with desire, not approach his wife when her courses appear; nor let him sleep with her in the same bed.

41. For the wisdom, the energy, the strength, the sight, and the vitality of a man who approaches a woman covered with menstrual excretions, utterly perish.

42. If he avoids her, while she is in that condition, his wisdom, energy, strength, sight, and vitality will increase.

43. Let him not eat in the company of his wife, nor look at her, while she eats, sneezes, yawns, or sits at her ease.

44. A Brahmana who desires energy must not look at (a woman) who applies collyrium to her eyes, has anointed or uncovered herself or brings forth (a child).

45. Let him not eat, dressed with one garment only; let him not bathe naked; let him not void urine on a road, on ashes, or in a cow-pen,

46. Nor on ploughed land, in water, on an altar of bricks, on a mountain, on the ruins of a temple, nor ever on an ant-hill,

47. Nor in holes inhabited by living creatures, nor while he walks or stands, nor on reaching the bank of a river, nor on the top of a mountain.

48. Let him never void faeces or urine, facing the wind, or a fire, or looking towards a Brahmana, the sun, water, or cows.

49. He may ease himself, having covered (the ground) with sticks, clods, leaves, grass, and the like, restraining his speech, (keeping himself) pure, wrapping up his body, and covering his head.

50. Let him void faeces and urine, in the daytime turning to the north, at night turning towards the south, during the two twilights in the same (position) as by day.

51. In the shade or in darkness a Brahmana may, both by day and at night, do it, assuming any position he pleases; likewise when his life is in danger.

52. The intellect of (a man) who voids urine against a fire, the sun, the moon, in water, against a Brahmana, a cow, or the wind, perishes.

53. Let him not blow a fire with his mouth; let him not look at a naked woman; let him not throw any impure substance into the fire, and let him not warm his feet at it.

54. Let him not place (fire) under (a bed or the like); nor step over it, nor place it (when he sleeps) at the foot-(end of his bed); let him not torment living creatures.

55. Let him not eat, nor travel, nor sleep during the twilight; let him not scratch the ground; let him not take off his garland.

11 CHAPTER 5

146. Thus the rules of personal purification for men of all castes, and those for cleaning (inanimate) things, have been fully declared to you: hear now the duties of women.

147. By a girl, by a young woman, or even by an aged one, nothing must be done independently, even in her own house.

148. In childhood a female must be subject to her father, in youth to her husband, when her lord is dead to her sons; a woman must never be independent.

149. She must not seek to separate herself from her father, husband, or sons; by leaving them she would make both (her own and her husband's) families contemptible.

150. She must always be cheerful, clever in (the management of her) household affairs, careful in cleaning her utensils, and economical in expenditure.

151. Him to whom her father may give her, or her brother with the father's permission, she shall obey as long as he lives, and when he is dead, she must not insult (his memory).

152. For the sake of procuring good fortune to (brides), the recitation of benedictory texts (svastyayana), and the sacrifice to the Lord of creatures (Pragapati) are used at weddings; (but) the betrothal (by the father or guardian) is the cause of (the husband's) dominion (over his wife).

153. The husband who wedded her with sacred texts, always gives happiness to his wife, both in season and out of season, in this world and in the next.

154. Though destitute of virtue, or seeking pleasure (elsewhere), or devoid of good qualities, (yet) a husband must be constantly worshipped as a god by a faithful wife.

155. No sacrifice, no vow, no fast must be performed by women apart (from their husbands); if a wife obeys her husband, she will for that (reason alone) be exalted in heaven.

156. A faithful wife, who desires to dwell (after death) with her husband, must never do anything that might displease him who took her hand, whether he be alive or dead.

157. At her pleasure let her emaciate her body by (living on) pure flowers, roots, and fruit; but she must never even mention the name of another man after her husband has died.

158. Until death let her be patient (of hardships), self-controlled, and chaste, and strive (to fulfil) that most excellent duty which (is prescribed) for wives who have one husband only.

159. Many thousands of Brahmanas who were chaste from their youth, have gone to heaven without continuing their race.

160. A virtuous wife who after the death of her husband constantly remains chaste, reaches heaven, though she have no son, just like those chaste men.

161. But a woman who from a desire to have offspring violates her duty towards her (deceased) husband, brings on herself disgrace in this world, and loses her place with her husband (in heaven).

162. Offspring begotten by another man is here not (considered lawful), nor (does offspring begotten) on another man's wife (belong to the begetter), nor is a second husband anywhere prescribed for virtuous women.

163. She who cohabits with a man of higher caste, forsaking her own husband who belongs to a lower one, will become contemptible in this world, and is called a remarried woman (parapurva).

164. By violating her duty towards her husband, a wife is disgraced in this world, (after death) she enters the womb of a jackal, and is tormented by diseases (the punishment of) her sin.

165. She who, controlling her thoughts, words, and deeds, never slights her lord, resides (after death) with her husband (in heaven), and is called a virtuous (wife).

166. In reward of such conduct, a female who controls her thoughts, speech, and actions, gains in this (life) highest renown, and in the next (world) a place near her husband.

167. A twice-born man, versed in the sacred law, shall burn a wife of equal caste who conducts herself thus and dies before him, with (the sacred fires used for) the Agnihotra, and with the sacrificial implements.

168. Having thus, at the funeral, given the sacred fires to his wife who dies before him, he may marry again, and again kindle (the fires).

169. (Living) according to the (preceding) rules, he must never neglect the five (great) sacrifices, and, having taken a wife, he must dwell in (his own) house during the second period of his life.

12 CHAPTERS 6 AND 7: DUTIES OF RETIREMENT AND DUTIES OF THE KING.

1. A twice-born Snataka, who has thus lived according to the law in the order of householders, may, taking a firm resolution and keeping his organs in subjection, dwell in the forest, duly (observing the rules given below).

2. When a householder sees his (skin) wrinkled, and (his hair) white, and. the sons of his sons, then he may resort to the forest.

3. Abandoning all food raised by cultivation, and all his belongings, he may depart into the forest, either committing his wife to his sons, or accompanied by her.

36. Having studied the Vedas in accordance with the rule, having begat sons according to the sacred law, and having offered sacrifices according to his ability, he may direct his mind to (the attainment of) final liberation.

37. A twice-born man who seeks final liberation, without having studied the Vedas, without having begotten sons, and without having offered sacrifices, sinks downwards.

Chapter 7:

144. The highest duty of a Kshatriya is to protect his subjects, for the king who enjoys the rewards, just mentioned, is bound to (discharge that) duty.

145. Having risen in the last watch of the night, having performed (the rite of) personal purification, having, with a collected mind, offered oblations in the fire, and having worshipped Brahmanas, he shall enter the hall of audience which must possess the marks (considered) auspicious (for a dwelling).

146. Tarrying there, he shall gratify all subjects (who come to see him by a kind reception) and afterwards dismiss them; having dismissed his subjects, he shall take counsel with his ministers.

147. Ascending the back of a hill or a terrace, (and) retiring (there) in a lonely place, or in a solitary forest, let him consult with them unobserved.

148. That king whose secret plans other people, (though) assembled (for the purpose), do not discover, (will) enjoy the whole earth, though he be poor in treasure.

149. At the time of consultation let him cause to be removed idiots, the dumb, the blind, and the deaf, animals, very aged men, women, barbarians, the sick, and those deficient in limbs.

150. (Such) despicable (persons), likewise animals, and particularly women betray secret council; for that reason he must be careful with respect to them.

151. At midday or at midnight, when his mental and bodily fatigues are over, let him deliberate, either with himself alone or with his (ministers), on virtue, pleasure, and wealth,

152. On (reconciling) the attainment of these (aims) which are opposed to each other, on bestowing his daughters in marriage, and on keeping his sons (from harm),

153. On sending ambassadors, on the completion of undertakings (already begun), on the behaviour of (the women in) his harem, and on the doings of his spies.

154. On the whole eightfold business and the five classes (of spies), on the goodwill or enmity and the conduct of the circle (of neighbours he must) carefully (reflect).

13 CHAPTER 8: ON THE LEGAL SYSTEM AND ECONOMICS, PUNISHMENT AND TAXATION.

61. I will fully declare what kind of men may be made witnesses in suits by creditors, and in what manner those (witnesses) must give true (evidence).

62. Householders, men with male issue, and indigenous (inhabitants of the country, be they) Kshatriyas, Vaisyas, or Sudras, are competent, when called by a suitor, to give evidence, not any persons whatever (their condition may be) except in cases of urgency.

68. Women should give evidence for women, and for twice-born men twice-born men (of the) same (kind), virtuous Sudras for Sudras, and men of the lowest castes for the lowest.

197. If anybody sells the property of another man, without being the owner and without the assent of the owner, the (judge) shall not admit him who is a thief, though he may not consider himself as a thief, as a witness (in any case).

198. If the (offender) is a kinsman (of the owner), he shall be fined six hundred panas; if he is not a kinsman, nor has any excuse, he shall be guilty of theft.

199. A gift or sale, made by anybody else but the owner, must be considered as null and void, according to the rule in judicial proceedings.

200. Where possession is evident, but no title is perceived, there the title (shall be) a proof (of ownership), not possession; such is the settled rule.

201. He who obtains a chattel in the market before a number (of witnesses), acquires that chattel with a clear legal title by purchase.

202. If the original (seller) be not producible, (the buyer) being exculpated by a public sale, must be dismissed by the king without punishment, but (the former owner) who lost the chattel shall receive it (back from the buyer).

203. One commodity mixed with another must not be sold (as pure), nor a bad one (as good), nor less (than the proper quantity or weight), nor anything that is not at hand or that is concealed.

204. If, after one damsel has been shown, another be given to the bridegroom, he may marry them both for the same price; that Manu ordained.

205. He who gives (a damsel in marriage), having first openly declared her blemishes, whether she be insane, or afflicted with leprosy, or have lost her virginity, is not liable to punishment.

352. Men who commit adultery with the wives of others, the king shall cause to be marked by punishments which cause terror, and afterwards banish.

353. For by (adultery) is caused a mixture of the castes (varna) among men; thence (follows) sin, which cuts up even the roots and causes the destruction of everything.

354. A man formerly accused of (such) offences, who secretly converses with another man's wife, shall pay the first (or lowest) amercement.

355. But a man, not before accused, who (thus) speaks with (a woman) for some (reasonable) cause, shall not incur any guilt, since in him there is no transgression.

356. He who addresses the wife of another man at a Tirtha, outside the village, in a forest, or at the confluence of rivers, suffer (the punishment for) adulterous acts (samgrahana).

357. Offering presents (to a woman), romping (with her), touching her ornaments and dress, sitting with her on a bed, all (these acts) are considered adulterous acts (samgrahana).

358. If one touches a woman in a place (which ought) not (to be touched) or allows (oneself to be touched in such a spot), all (such acts done) with mutual consent are declared (to be) adulterous (samgrahana).

359. A man who is not a Brahmana ought to suffer death for adultery (samgrahana); for the wives of all the four castes even must always be carefully guarded.

360. Mendicants, bards, men who have performed the initiatory ceremony of a Vedic sacrifice, and artisans are not prohibited from speaking to married women.

361. Let no man converse with the wives of others after he has been forbidden (to do so); but he who converses (with them), in spite of a prohibition, shall be fined one suvarna.

362. This rule does not apply to the wives of actors and singers, nor (of) those who live on (the intrigues of) their own (wives); for such men send their wives (to others) or, concealing themselves, allow them to hold criminal intercourse.

363. Yet he who secretly converses with such women, or with female slaves kept by one (master), and with female ascetics, shall be compelled to pay a small fine.

364. He who violates an unwilling maiden shall instantly suffer corporal punishment; but a man who enjoys a willing maiden shall not suffer corporal punishment, if (his caste be) the same (as hers).

365. From a maiden who makes advances to a (man of) high (caste), he shall not take any fine; but her, who courts a (man of) low (caste), let him force to live confined in her house.

366. A (man of) low (caste) who makes love to a maiden (of) the highest (caste) shall suffer corporal punishment; he who addresses a maiden (on) equal (caste) shall pay the nuptial fee, if her father desires it.

367. But if any man through insolence forcibly contaminates a maiden, two of his fingers shall be instantly cut off, and he shall pay a fine of six hundred (panas).

368. A man (of) equal (caste) who defiles a willing maiden shall not suffer the amputation of his fingers, but shall pay a fine of two hundred (panas) in order to deter him from a repetition (of the offence).

369. A damsel who pollutes (another) damsel must be fined two hundred (panas), pay the double of her (nuptial) fee, and receive ten (lashes with a) rod.

370. But a woman who pollutes a damsel shall instantly have (her head) shaved or two fingers cut off, and be made to ride (through the town) on a donkey.

371. If a wife, proud of the greatness of her relatives or (her own) excellence, violates the duty which she owes to her lord, the king shall cause her to be devoured by dogs in a place frequented by many.

372. Let him cause the male offender to be burnt on a red-hot iron bed; they shall put logs under it, (until) the sinner is burned (to death).

373. On a man (once) convicted, who is (again) accused within a year, a double fine (must be inflicted); even thus (must the fine be doubled) for (repeated) intercourse with a Vratya and a Kandali.

374. A Sudra who has intercourse with a woman of a twice-born caste (varna), guarded or unguarded, (shall be punished in the following manner): if she was unguarded,

he loses the part (offending) and all his property; if she was guarded, everything (even his life).

375. (For intercourse with a guarded Brahmana a Vaisya shall forfeit all his property after imprisonment for a year; a Kshatriya shall be fined one thousand (panas) and be shaved with the urine (of an ass).

376. If a Vaisya or a Kshatriya has connexion with an unguarded Brahmana, let him fine the Vaisya five hundred (panas) and the Kshatriya one thousand.

377. But even these two, if they offend with a Brahmani (not only) guarded (but the wife of an eminent man), shall be punished like a Sudra or be burnt in a fire of dry grass.

378. A Brahmana who carnally knows a guarded Brahmani against her will, shall be fined one thousand (panas); but he shall be made to pay five hundred, if he had connexion with a willing one.

379. Tonsure (of the head) is ordained for a Brahmana (instead of) capital punishment; but (men of) other castes shall suffer capital punishment.

380. Let him never slay a Brahmana, though he have committed all (possible) crimes; let him banish such an (offender), leaving all his property (to him) and (his body) unhurt.

381. No greater crime is known on earth than slaying a Brahmana; a king, therefore, must not even conceive in his mind the thought of killing a Brahmana.

382. If a Vaisya approaches a guarded female of the Kshatriya caste, or a Kshatriya a (guarded) Vaisya woman, they both deserve the same punishment as in the case of an unguarded Brahmana female.

383. A Brahmana shall be compelled to pay a fine of one thousand (panas) if he has intercourse with guarded (females of) those two (castes); for (offending with) a (guarded) Sudra female a fine of one thousand (panas shall be inflicted) on a Kshatriya or a Vaisya.

384. For (intercourse with) an unguarded Kshatriya a fine of five hundred (panas shall fall) on a Vaisya; but (for the same offence) a Kshatriya shall be shaved with the urine (of a donkey) or (pay) the same fine.

385. A Brahmana who approaches unguarded females (of the) Kshatriya or Vaisya (castes), or a Sudra female, shall be fined five hundred (panas); but (for intercourse with) a female (of the) lowest (castes), one thousand.

386. That king in whose town lives no thief, no adulterer, no defamer, no man guilty of violence, and no committer of assaults, attains the world of Sakra (Indra).

14 CHAPTER 9: ON WOMEN, MARRIAGE, AND THE KINDS OF MARRIAGE.

1. I will now propound the eternal laws for a husband and his wife who keep to the path of duty, whether they be united or separated.

2. Day and night woman must be kept in dependence by the males (of) their (families), and, if they attach themselves to sensual enjoyments, they must be kept under one's control.

3. Her father protects (her) in childhood, her husband protects (her) in youth, and her sons protect (her) in old age; a woman is never fit for independence.

4. Reprehensible is the father who gives not (his daughter in marriage) at the proper time; reprehensible is the husband who approaches not (his wife in due season), and reprehensible is the son who does not protect his mother after her husband has died.

5. Women must particularly be guarded against evil inclinations, however trifling (they may appear); for, if they are not guarded, they will bring sorrow on two families.

6. Considering that the highest duty of all castes, even weak husbands (must) strive to guard their wives.

7. He who carefully guards his wife, preserves (the purity of) his offspring, virtuous conduct, his family, himself, and his (means of acquiring) merit.

8. The husband, after conception by his wife, becomes an embryo and is born again of her; for that is the wifehood of a wife (gaya), that he is born (gayate) again by her.

9. As the male is to whom a wife cleaves, even so is the son whom she brings forth; let him therefore carefully guard his wife, in order to keep his offspring pure.

10. No man can completely guard women by force; but they can be guarded by the employment of the (following) expedients:

11. Let the (husband) employ his (wife) in the collection and expenditure of his wealth, in keeping (everything) clean, in (the fulfilment of) religious duties, in the preparation of his food, and in looking after the household utensils.

12. Women, confined in the house under trustworthy and obedient servants, are not (well) guarded; but those who of their own accord keep guard over themselves, are well guarded.

13. Drinking (spirituous liquor), associating with wicked people, separation from the husband, rambling abroad, sleeping (at unseasonable hours), and dwelling in other men's houses, are the six causes of the ruin of women.

14. Women do not care for beauty, nor is their attention fixed on age; (thinking), '(It is enough that) he is a man,' they give themselves to the handsome and to the ugly.

15. Through their passion for men, through their mutable temper, through their natural heartlessness, they become disloyal towards their husbands, however carefully they may be guarded in this (world).

16. Knowing their disposition, which the Lord of creatures laid in them at the creation, to be such, (every) man should most strenuously exert himself to guard them.

17. (When creating them) Manu allotted to women (a love of their) bed, (of their) seat and (of) ornament, impure desires, wrath, dishonesty, malice, and bad conduct.

18. For women no (sacramental) rite (is performed) with sacred texts, thus the law is settled; women (who are) destitute of strength and destitute of (the knowledge of) Vedic texts, (are as impure as) falsehood (itself), that is a fixed rule.

19. And to this effect many sacred texts are sung also in the Vedas, in order to (make) fully known the true disposition (of women); hear (now those texts which refer to) the expiation of their (sins).

20. 'If my mother, going astray and unfaithful, conceived illicit desires, may my father keep that seed from me,' that is the scriptural text.

21. If a woman thinks in her heart of anything that would pain her husband, the (above-mentioned text) is declared (to be a means for) completely removing such infidelity.

22. Whatever be the qualities of the man with whom a woman is united according to the law, such qualities even she assumes, like a river (united) with the ocean.

23. Akshamala, a woman of the lowest birth, being united to Vasishtha and Sarangi, (being united) to Mandapala, became worthy of honour.

24. These and other females of low birth have attained eminence in this world by the respective good qualities of their husbands.

25. Thus has been declared the ever pure popular usage (which regulates the relations) between husband and wife; hear (next) the laws concerning children which are the cause of happiness in this world and after death.

26. Between wives (striyah) who (are destined) to bear children, who secure many blessings, who are worthy of worship and irradiate (their) dwellings, and between the goddesses of fortune (sriyah, who reside) in the houses (of men), there is no difference whatsoever.

27. The production of children, the nurture of those born, and the daily life of men, (of these matters) woman is visibly the cause.

28. Offspring, (the due performance on religious rites, faithful service, highest conjugal happiness and heavenly bliss for the ancestors and oneself, depend on one's wife alone.

29. She who, controlling her thoughts, speech, and acts, violates not her duty towards her lord, dwells with him (after death) in heaven, and in this world is called by the virtuous a faithful (wife, sadhvi)

30. But for disloyalty to her husband a wife is censured among men, and (in her next life) she is born in the womb of a jackal and tormented by diseases, the punishment of her sin.

31. Listen (now) to the following holy discussion, salutary to all men, which the virtuous (of the present day) and the ancient great sages have held concerning male offspring.

32. They (all) say that the male issue (of a woman) belongs to the lord, but with respect to the (meaning of the term) lord the revealed texts differ; some call the begetter (of the child the lord), others declare (that it is) the owner of the soil.

33. By the sacred tradition the woman is declared to be the soil, the man is declared to be the seed; the production of all corporeal beings (takes place) through the union of the soil with the seed.

34. In some cases the seed is more distinguished, and in some the womb of the female; but when both are equal, the offspring is most highly esteemed.

35. On comparing the seed and the receptacle (of the seed), the seed is declared to be more important; for the offspring of all created beings is marked by the characteristics of the seed.

36. Whatever (kind on seed is sown in a field, prepared in due season, (a plant) of that same kind, marked with the peculiar qualities of the seed, springs up in it.

37. This earth, indeed, is called the primeval womb of created beings; but the seed develops not in its development any properties of the womb.

38. In this world seeds of different kinds, sown at the proper time in the land, even in one field, come forth (each) according to its kind.

39. The rice (called) vrihi and (that called) sali, mudga-beans, sesamum, masha-beans, barley, leeks, and sugar-cane, (all) spring up according to their seed.

40. That one (plant) should be sown and another be produced cannot happen; whatever seed is sown, (a plant of) that kind even comes forth.

41. Never therefore must a prudent well-trained man, who knows the Veda and its Angas and desires long life, cohabit with another's wife.

42. With respect to this (matter), those acquainted with the past recite some stanzas, sung by Vayu (the Wind, to show) that seed must not be sown by (any) man on that which belongs to another.

ABOUT THE AUTHOR

O₂pen Windows: A Feminist Resource and Research Center.

O₂pen Windows is a feminist research cum *adda* center, based in Bangalore. If it could, it would sustain itself with endless cups of tea and lots of stimulating research.

The Purpose: O₂pen Windows encourages research on both contemporary and historical socio-cultural issues and literary issues. These findings will subsequently be documented, archived and published as monographs and essays.

For more information, write to: openwindows101@gmail.com.

VISIT US AT: www.aresourcecenter.wordpress.com.